WHAT'S YOUR STORY, FREDERICK DOUGLASS?

Jody Jensen Shaffer
illustrations by Doug Jones

Lerner Publications ◆ Minneapolis

Note to readers, parents, and educators:
This book includes an interview of a famous American. While the words this person speaks are not his actual words, all the information in the book is true and has been carefully researched.

Lerner Publications Company
A division of Lerner Publishing Group, Inc.
241 First Avenue North
Minneapolis, MN 55401 USA

For reading levels and more information, look up this title at www.lernerbooks.com.

Main body text set in Avenir LT Pro 45 Book 15/21. Typeface provided by Linotype AG.

Library of Congress Cataloging-in-Publication Data

Shaffer, Jody Jensen.
    What's your story, Frederick Douglass? / by Jody Jensen Shaffer.
        pages cm. – (Cub reporter meets famous Americans)
    Includes index.
    ISBN 978-1-4677-8784-0 (lb : alk. paper)—ISBN 978-1-4677-9647-7
(pb : alk. paper)—ISBN 978-1-4677-9648-4 (eb pdf)
    1. Douglass, Frederick, 1818–1895—Juvenile literature. 2. Abolitionists—United States—Biography—Juvenile literature. 3. African American abolitionists—Biography—Juvenile literature. 4. Antislavery movements—United States—Juvenile literature. I. Title.
E449.D75S53 2016
973.8092—dc23 [B]   2015013844

Manufactured in the United States of America
1 – VP – 12/31/15

Table of Contents

Hello, everybody! Today I'm speaking with a very important person from history. His name is Frederick Douglass. Frederick, can you tell us about yourself?

Frederick says: Certainly. I was born at a time in the United States when most black people had no rights. In fact, many black people were forced to work for white people without pay. This was called **slavery**. Slaves had to do whatever they were told. Most slaves worked on farms in the South. Slavery was not legal in the North. Slaves could not own property or vote. They were not allowed to go to school. But I taught myself to read and write. When I grew up, I started a newspaper. I gave speeches about **abolishing**, or ending, slavery. I even gave advice to presidents.

Frederick lived much of his life in slavery. He spent his adult life speaking out against slavery.

When and where were you born?

Frederick says: I was born in February of 1818 on a **plantation** in Tuckahoe, Maryland. My mother named me Frederick Augustus Washington Bailey. Many slaves lived on plantations at that time. We planted and **harvested** crops. We did other kinds of hard work too.

Growing up, I did not know my mother well. I saw her only a few times when I was little. That's because she was taken from me when I was a baby. She was sent to work on a different plantation. Parents who were slaves were often separated from their children. My grandmother and grandfather raised me. They took care of all of their grandchildren, so I had lots of other kids to play with.

Slaves harvest sweet potatoes on a plantation in South Carolina in 1862. Like these slaves, Frederick and his family were forced to work on someone else's land.

What was your childhood like?

Frederick says: I enjoyed living with my grandparents, brothers and sisters, and cousins. The kids in my family used our imaginations a lot since we didn't have many toys to play with. We played outside and caught fish for dinner. We all lived together in a small log hut. I learned later that our home belonged to Aaron Anthony, the white man who owned us.

Frederick lived in a small log cabin like this one.

Some slave families, such as this one, were separated when owners sold slaves to other plantations. Frederick's mother was sold to another farm when Frederick was young.

What did you think about being a slave?

Frederick says: I didn't know I was a slave until I was seven. I found out when Aaron Anthony sent me to live in a house on a different piece of land he owned. It was then I realized that Aaron Anthony owned my family and me, and he could send us wherever he wanted. That made me angry.

My grandmother walked 12 miles (19 kilometers) with me to the house where I was to live. Aaron Anthony lived there too. My grandmother had to leave me with Aaron Anthony and return to the cabin where I'd lived with her. I cried myself to sleep that night. I missed my family and my home.

When Frederick was seven, his owner sent him to live in another house *(above)*. After moving here, Frederick never saw his grandmother again.

What happened after you were sent away?

Frederick says: I didn't live in my new home for long. When I was eight, I was sent to Baltimore, Maryland, to live with a couple named Sophia and Hugh Auld. I took care of the Aulds' two-year-old son, Tommy. Sophia Auld started teaching me to read. But soon, her husband made her stop. He believed that slaves shouldn't learn to read. And, in fact, teaching slaves to read was against the law in Maryland. But I knew I wanted to learn how to read. So I started carrying a spelling book with me when I ran errands. I asked white children to help me read it and gave them biscuits if they agreed. After I'd learned enough to read by myself, I read everything I could get my hands on.

In Frederick's time, many children learned to read from books that looked like this.

As runs the Glass,
Our Life doth pass.

My Book and Heart,
Must never part.

Job feels the Rod,
Yet blesses GOD.

Proud Korah's Troop,
Was swallowed up.

Lot fled to Zoar,
Saw fiery Shower
On Sodom pour.

Moses was he,
Who Israel's Host
Led thro' the Sea.

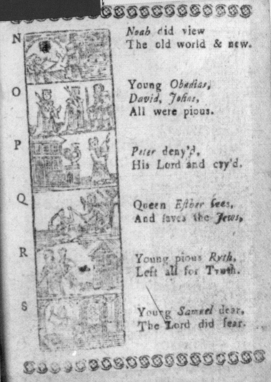

Noah did view
The old world & new.

Young Obadias,
David, Josias,
All were pious.

Peter deny'd,
His Lord and cry'd.

Queen Esther fees,
And faves the Jews.

Young pious Ruth,
Left all for Truth.

Young Samuel dear,
The Lord did fear.

How long did you live in Baltimore?

Frederick says: I lived there for seven years. When I was fifteen, I went to live with Thomas Auld, Hugh's brother. But we didn't get along, so Thomas sent me to the country to work for a man named Edward Covey. On my way there, I decided I would escape from slavery someday. I hated moving around, and I hated not being able to choose where I lived.

In the country, I was beaten and nearly starved. Edward Covey hurt me many times. I fought back to defend myself, and he finally backed down. But I knew I had to get away and find a better life.

Thomas Auld *(above)* hired Frederick out to another man, Edward Covey. Frederick wanted freedom from slavery.

How did you escape slavery?

Frederick says: I started talking to other slaves. Together, we made a plan to break free in April 1836. Our plan was to take a canoe and escape on the Chesapeake Bay. But before we could escape, another slave told on us. We were sent to jail.

Eventually, I was sent back to Baltimore to live with Hugh and Sophia Auld. By this time, Aaron Anthony had died and Hugh Auld had officially claimed me as his slave. In 1838, I dressed like a sailor and escaped to New York City. At last, I was living in a state that did not have slavery.

There was another big change in my life at this time too. I met a woman named Anna Murray, and we fell in love. We got married and moved to New Bedford, Massachusetts. There we changed our last name to Douglass so that my owner couldn't easily find me.

Frederick *(left)* married Anna Murray *(below)* in 1838. Anna was free. But Frederick was not. He had to be careful not to get caught and sent back to his owner.

What was your life like in New Bedford?

Frederick says: It was busy. Some parts were good, but other parts were hard. Anna and I started a family. I traveled and gave speeches against slavery. I also wrote a book about my life. It was called *Narrative of the Life of Frederick Douglass, an American Slave, Written by Himself.*

Anna and I were happy, but we worried that I would be found and returned to my master. I worried even more after the book came out. It was safer for an escaped slave to stay quiet and not speak out. Yet I felt that speaking out was important. I wanted to share the story of my life.

This is a page from Frederick's book. This story has taught people a lot about Frederick and his life as a slave.

NARRATIVE

OF THE

LIFE

OF

FREDERICK DOUGLASS,

AN

AMERICAN SLAVE.

WRITTEN BY HIMSELF.

BOSTON:
PUBLISHED AT THE ANTI-SLAVERY OFFICE,
No. 25 Cornhill.
1845.

Frederick Douglass

How did you stay safe after your book came out?

Frederick says: I decided to go to Great Britain. Slavery didn't exist there. I could be truly free. I loved the freedom in Great Britain. But Anna was still in the United States. I missed her and the rest of my family. If I went back, Hugh Auld could capture me. He could make me a slave again. So some of my friends raised some money. They bought me my freedom from Hugh Auld. In December of 1846, I became a free man and moved back to the United States to be with my family.

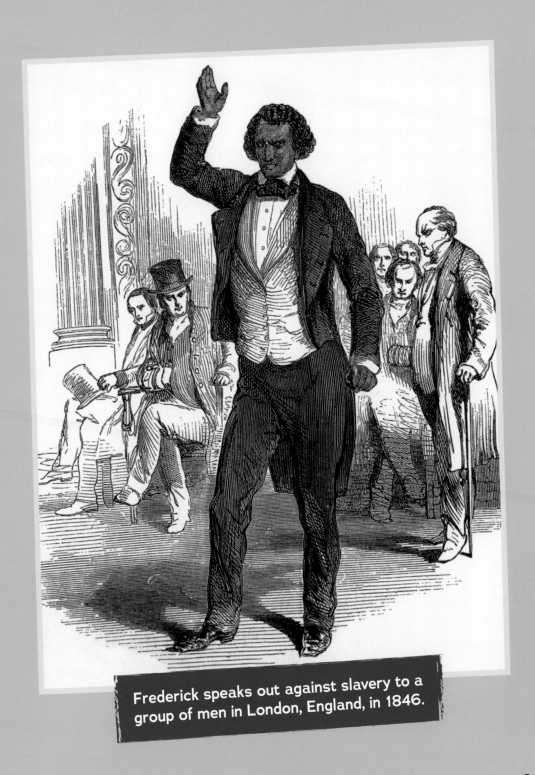

Frederick speaks out against slavery to a group of men in London, England, in 1846.

What did you do to try to end slavery when you got back to the United States?

Frederick says: My family moved to Rochester, New York, a town with many antislavery groups. I continued speaking out against slavery and talking about why everyone should be treated equally. My home became a stop on the **Underground Railroad**. The Underground Railroad wasn't a real railroad. Instead, it was a system made up of people like me who wanted slavery to end. We offered our homes as stops along the way from slave states to free states. Escaping slaves could hide and rest in these homes as they made their way north.

Frederick once lived in this house in Rochester, New York. It was a stop along the Underground Railroad.

Did your hard work finally help to end slavery?

Frederick says: It did, but not as quickly as I hoped. And the country went through some hard times before slavery came to an end. In 1860, Abraham Lincoln was elected president. He was against slavery. That made me and many others happy, but it made lots of people in the southern states mad. Eleven southern states formed a new nation called the **Confederacy**. They didn't want to be part of the United States if slavery wouldn't be allowed there. A war began between the Confederacy and the North. This was called the Civil War (1861–1865). In 1865, the North won the war. Around the same time, President Lincoln was killed, but others took over his work to end slavery for good.

Abraham Lincoln was president during the Civil War. The war was fought partly to end slavery in the United States.

What did you do after the Civil War?

Frederick says: I kept talking to people about **civil rights**. Even after slavery ended, black people still didn't have the same freedoms as white people. I made speeches about black people getting the right to vote. I advised government leaders about issues that were important to black people. And I spoke against the **black codes**. These laws allowed black people to still be treated as slaves. I had also started my own newspaper called the *North Star*, and I kept up my work on that. The *North Star* included antislavery articles. I hoped that if more people heard me talking about equality, they might join me in the fight for fairness.

This photograph of Frederick was taken around 1880.

How did your work make a difference?

Frederick says: I was America's first black civil rights leader. I was able to use my voice and my pen to improve life for blacks in both the North and the South. I worked hard at this goal because I believed in it so deeply. Everyone deserves to be treated equally, no matter who they are or where they come from.

Timeline

1818 Frederick Douglass is born Frederick Augustus Washington Bailey in Tuckahoe, Maryland.

1825 Frederick learns that his mother has died.

1826 Frederick is sent to Baltimore, Maryland, to live with the Auld family, where he learns to read.

1833 Frederick is sent to work for Thomas Auld in Saint Michaels, Maryland.

1834 Frederick is sent to work for Edward Covey.

1838 Frederick escapes to New York City and then moves to Rochester, New York, where he marries Anna Murray, and they change their last name to Douglass.

1845 Frederick publishes his first autobiography, *Narrative of the Life of Frederick Douglass, an American Slave, Written by Himself.*

1846 Frederick goes to England, Scotland, and Ireland to speak against slavery. His friends buy his freedom.

1847 Frederick returns to Rochester, New York, and starts a newspaper called the *North Star.*

1895 Frederick dies at his home, Cedar Hill, in Washington, DC.

Glossary

abolishing: officially putting an end to something

black codes: laws passed by southern states to limit the freedom of black people

civil rights: the rights of every person to work, vote, own property, learn, and live

Confederacy: another name for the Confederate States of America. These were eleven southern states that left the United States to keep slavery and states' rights.

harvested: picked food from plants

plantation: a huge estate on which crops such as cotton and tobacco are grown and on which slaves worked

slavery: the practice of one human being owning another

Underground Railroad: a network of secret routes and houses used by black slaves who were escaping to freedom in the North

LERNER

Expand learning beyond the printed book. Download free, complementary educational resources for this book from our website, www.lernerresource.com.

SOURCE

Further Information

Books

Barton, Jen. *What's Your Story, Harriet Tubman?* Minneapolis: Lerner Publications, 2016. This book introduces young readers to Harriet Tubman, another important figure in the fight against slavery.

Coleman, Wim, and Pat Perrin. *A Slave's Education in Courage: The Life of Frederick Douglass.* South Egremont, MA: Red Chair, 2015. This play is adapted from Douglass's third autobiography.

Slade, Suzanne. *Friends for Freedom: The Story of Susan B. Anthony & Frederick Douglass.* Watertown, MA: Charlesbridge, 2014. This is a story of two unlikely friends with common goals.

Websites

NPS: Frederick Douglass—National Historic Site
http://www.nps.gov/frdo/learn/kidsyouth/index.htm
This website contains facts about Frederick Douglass's final home, Cedar Hill.

PBS Video—*Who Is Frederick Douglass?*
http://video.pbs.org/video/2319979061
This short video explores Frederick Douglass's life and work.

Index

Photo Acknowledgments

The images in this book are used with the permission of: © Hulton Archive/Getty Images, p. 5; © H P Moore/ Getty Images, p. 7; Library of Congress, pp. 9 (top), 13, 25; © MPI/Getty Images, pp. 9 (bottom), 27; Maryland State Archives, pp. 11, 15; © Fotosearch/ Getty Images, p. 17 (top); Wikimedia Commons, cc 3.0, p. 17 (bottom); © Newberry Library/Bridgeman Images, p. 19; © CORBIS, p. 21; © Rochester County Library, p. 23.

Front cover: © Bettmann/CORBIS.